Salmon Matters

How a Fish Feeds a Forest

Lisa Connors
illustrated by Betty Gatewood

Salmon Matters

How a Fish Feeds a Forest

Written by Lisa Connors

Illustrated by Betty Gatewood

To Chris, again. *lmc*

To Michael Pelton, Karen Lutz, Dennis Dechene, Paul Bugas, and Virginia Department of Game and Inland Fisheries for access to black bear mounted specimens, plus grizzly bear, bald eagle and alevin photographs. Also to Lisa for her amazing confidence in my art, and to my husband Mark for his constant support. *BG*

No part of this publication may be reproduced in whole or in part, or stored in a retrieval system or transmitted in any form or by any means, electronic, mechanical, photocopying, recording, or otherwise without prior permission of the author.

The illustrations in this book were done in watercolor.

Text copyright@2018 by Lisa Connors
Illustrations copyright @ 2018 by Betty Gatewood
All Rights Reserved

Fish live in water and trees live in soil on land. Trees get their energy to grow from the sun, but also from nutrients, such as nitrogen. These nutrients come from dead plants and animals that lived in the forest.

When they died, decomposers broke down their bodies and returned these nutrients to the soil.

We could say that forest animals and plants feed the trees. Scientists have learned that in the Pacific Northwest, salmon feed the trees. How can a fish feed a forest? Let's start with a look at their life cycle.

Each year in late fall, coho salmon migrate from the Pacific Ocean to the river where they were born years ago. Females find a gravel bed, called a redd, and build their nests with small pebbles. Males fertilize the eggs. This is called spawning. The adult fish guard their eggs for about twelve days. Then the adults die. Their lives are over, but the salmon life cycle continues.

In early winter, tiny baby salmon called alevin hatch.

For many weeks they hide in the gravel for safety, getting nourishment from the yolk sac of their eggs.

Once the yolk sac is used up, the young salmon must find their own food. They explore the creek searching for insect larvae. In this stage of their life they are called fry.

The fry stay in the creek eating and growing for about a year. The following spring they have an instinctual urge to migrate to the ocean. Their bodies change as they go, allowing them to live in salt water once they reach the sea. Now the salmon are called smolts.

Someday they'll return home to spawn and to feed the forest.

In the ocean, coho eat zooplankton, crustaceans such as shrimp and krill, mollusks, squid and small fish. Adult salmon live and feed in the ocean for about eighteen months. Then instinct calls again. It's time to go home.

Just like their parents, they'll struggle on a dramatic migration of up to 900 miles and more than 6,000 feet of elevation. They'll swim against the current, encounter obstacles and fend off exhaustion and predators. It's an amazing feat.

Just like their parents, they'll find a mate, lay and protect their eggs, and then die.

But that's not all.

Many animals come to the stream when salmon spawn. Bald eagles, otters, wolves, martens, ravens, gulls and crows all eat salmon. These animals get energy from the salmon to grow and complete their life cycles.

Bears especially have been waiting for this day. They've been eating mostly insects and fruit since they emerged from hibernation. Now, their favorite food has arrived.

But that's not all.

When grizzly and black bears feed, they often carry fish up to 150 meters into the forest to eat alone. If there are a lot of fish spawning, bears only eat the eggs and brain, the parts with the most fat. Bears need to gain weight before hibernation. They leave the rest of the fish and return to the stream for more.

The fish bodies are not wasted. Crows and ravens will eat from the bear's leftovers.

Forest decomposers also use the dead fish. Flies lay eggs in the decaying salmon. In just a few days a dead salmon will be full of wriggling maggots.

The fly larvae crawl into the ground for the winter. They pupate and emerge the following spring in time to feed warblers and flycatchers that just migrated from the south.

Other decomposers continue to break down the salmon bodies. Soon their nutrients such as nitrogen are available in the soil for plants to use. This nitrogen is a kind that comes from the ocean. The salmon brought it back in their bodies.

The salmon helped feed the forest!

But that's *still* not all.

Someday when the trees fall, they will decay and their nitrogen will enter the stream and be used by tiny plants and stream insects. And guess what?

Those plants and insects are what new salmon fry eat.

The salmon not only continue their own life cycles, they are tied to the life cycles of bears, birds, wolves, trees and small plants and insects that live in the streams. Salmon can feed us too. If we make sure they have the habitat to do so.

Want to know more?

This story is about coho salmon. There are other species of salmon. Each species is a little different in their life cycle. For example, how long they stay in the fry or smolt stage. However, they all migrate to sea and eventually return home to the streams of their birth.

Scientists often measure nitrogen (N) in habitats. The more common form of nitrogen found in terrestrial and freshwater habitats is called N14. But scientists discovered a different form of nitrogen called N15 in trees in the Pacific Northwest. N15 comes from plants and animals in the ocean. The salmon get this nitrogen from the food they eat while living in the ocean.

Salmon do not eat once they begin their spawning run. This means the nitrogen that their bodies give back to the land when they die all came from the ocean. Scientists realized how salmon were connected to the growth and life cycles of trees when they were measuring nitrogen in the trees near salmon streams. This discovery led to the understanding of how important bears are in spreading the nitrogen farther inland from the shoreline, making it available for trees to use. In areas where humans have chased out bears, the forests are less healthy.

Glossary

Alevin: a newly hatched trout or salmon with egg yolk still attached; sometimes called sac fry

Adult: the life cycle stage where an organism is able to mate and produce young

Estuary: a coastal body of water where streams meet the sea

Fry: the name used when the young salmon have used up their yolk-sac and can find food on their own

Invertebrate: an animal lacking a backbone

Larva: a life-cycle stage that occurs in insects that undergo complete metamorphosis

Migrate: to move from one habitat or region to another as part of seasonal patterns or in search of food

Milt: a fluid produced by the males of many aquatic organisms that contains sperm and is used to fertilize eggs

Nitrogen: a chemical element important for sustaining living organisms, and in which plants need to grow

Organism: a living being; an individual plant or animal

Redd: the spawning site or nest of some fish species

Smolt: a life-cycle stage where young salmon lose their camouflage stripes and undergo inside changes that allow them to live in saltwater

Smoltification: the process of undergoing internal changes, which allow a salmon to live in saltwater

Spawn: to release or deposit eggs

Bibliography

Baron, Nancy. "Salmon Trees." *Hakai Magazine*, Coastal Science and Societies, 15 Apr. 2015, www.hakaimagazine.com/features/salmon-trees/.

Gerdts, Jody, "Salmon in the trees: an assessment of a dendrochemical technique for detecting marine-derived nitrogen in riparian tree rings" (2012). WWU Masters Thesis Collection. 215. http://cedar.wwu.edu/wwuet/215

Reimchen, Thomas, and Caroline Fox. "Fine-Scale Spatiotemporal Influences of Salmon on Growth and Nitrogen Signatures of Sitka Spruce Tree Rings." *BMC Ecology*, vol. 13, no. 1, 2013, p. 38., doi:10.1186/1472-6785-13-38.

Stokes, M. Dale, and Doc White. *The Fish in the Forest: Salmon and the Web of Life.* University of California Press, 2014.

Temple, N. – editor: 2005. *Salmon in the Great Bear Rainforest.* Raincoast Conservation Society, Victoria, BC.

Meet the Author, Lisa Connors

Lisa loves exploring nature and writing stories. Best of all, she likes writing stories with nature in them. Her ideas often come from walks on her property in Virginia or from traveling with her husband Chris, a geologist. *Salmon Matters: How a Fish Feeds a Forest* uses the same **but that's not all** phrase used in her first book *Milkweed Matters: A Close Look at the Life Cycles within a Food Chain* to show how nature is connected. Lisa also wrote *Oliver's Otter Phase* (Arbordale Publishing, 2018). For more information, please visit her website: https://lisaconnors.wordpress.com

Meet the Illustrator, Betty Gatewood

Midway through her college career, Betty Gatewood changed her interest from laboratory science to the "outdoor" sciences of ecology and natural history; she's been outdoors ever since, teaching, learning, observing, painting. Betty is a retired middle school science teacher, former Teacher in Residence at Mary Baldwin University, and former Shenandoah National Park education/interpretive ranger. She pulls upon those experiences as she strives to paint a specimen or a scene with accuracy and detail, but also with emotion so the bigger story of the subject is understood by the observer.

Betty provided the cover art for Virginia's Mountain Treasures, published by The Wilderness Society, and for the Virginia Native Plant Society's Wildflower of the Year brochures for 2009, 2013 and 2018. She has contributed illustrations for the Appalachian Trail Conservancy's Appalachian Trail Adventure Book and Virginia Department of Forestry's book, Native Shrubs and Vines of Virginia. Her botanical illustrations, "Sycamore Trio" and "Wild Yam" won first and second place in the 2018 Virginia Outdoor Writers Association Excellence in Craft competition. She has conducted local art and journaling workshops for teachers, as well as Shenandoah National Park visitors. In 2016, her "Witch Hazel" botanical illustration was part of the National Park Service's Centennial exhibit at United States Botanic Garden in Washington, DC. She has also exhibited art at Staunton (Virginia) Public Library, Augusta County (Virginia) Library, and at Lewis Ginter Botanical Gardens in Richmond, Virginia. This is her second book to illustrate for author (and friend!) Lisa Connors. Their first collaborative project, *Milkweed Matters*, won awards in the 2017 Virginia Outdoor Writers Association Excellence in Craft competition. www.gatewoodgraphics.com

Made in the USA
Las Vegas, NV
15 March 2022

45709523R00021